T0148675

Who is *Love?*

MARY KAUFFMAN

WESTBOW®
PRESS
A DIVISION OF THOMAS NELSON
& ZONDERVAN

Scripture taken from the King James Version of the Bible.

Scripture taken from the Holy Bible, NEW INTERNATIONAL
VERSION®. Copyright © 1973, 1978, 1984 by Biblica, Inc.
All rights reserved worldwide. Used by permission. NEW
INTERNATIONAL VERSION® and NIV® are registered trademarks
of Biblica, Inc. Use of either trademark for the offering of goods or
services requires the prior written consent of Biblica US, Inc.

WestBow Press books may be ordered through booksellers or by contacting:

WestBow Press
A Division of Thomas Nelson & Zondervan
1663 Liberty Drive
Bloomington, IN 47403
www.westbowpress.com
1 (866) 928-1240

Because of the dynamic nature of the Internet, any web addresses or
links contained in this book may have changed since publication and
may no longer be valid. The views expressed in this work are solely those
of the author and do not necessarily reflect the views of the publisher,
and the publisher hereby disclaims any responsibility for them.

Any people depicted in stock imagery provided by Thinkstock are models,
and such images are being used for illustrative purposes only.
Certain stock imagery © Thinkstock.

ISBN: 978-1-4908-5567-7 (sc)
ISBN: 978-1-4908-5568-4 (e)

Library of Congress Control Number: 2014917870

Printed in the United States of America.

WestBow Press rev. date: 12/15/2014

Contents

About the Cover

The background is serene, peaceful and loving, which is the intent of this book. The butterfly is a symbol of transformation. The author's prayer is that many lives would be transformed into following Jesus. "And be not conformed to this world: but be ye transformed by the renewing of your mind, that ye may prove what is that good, and acceptable, and perfect, will of God." Romans 12:2 KJV

As a small child I remember enjoying the beauty and the amazement of the butterfly coming from an ugly cocoon. One day as I was thinking about so much evil in this world, a butterfly fluttered by. As I watched it I thought, that is God's way of saying "I love you and I'll always be with you." Now, whenever I see a butterfly, I'm always reminded of God and His love for me. Occasionally, He still sends a butterfly my way, what a blessing!

In Appreciation

In appreciation to my sons: Chuck, because he was the beginning inspiration to write this book, and an example to keep pressing forward, even through setbacks and rough times; and Ken, because of his deep spiritual insight and his willingness to share them with me, in our many endless talks. Also, thank you to Ray, my loving husband of fifty years, for his confidence in me to write a book and to encourage me to get it published. He has shown and taught me and our son's good work ethics.

Thanks to Rob, for still being a friend to Chuck through all the years, even with the long distance between the two of them. You made me realize a book like this could be helpful to many who have not had the same opportunities as I did in my childhood, being able to attend Sunday School and learning about Jesus at a very young age.

Thank you too, to Doris, Dan, Paul, Lois and others who helped to make this book possible.

Purpose

This book was written for a very definite purpose – to help those who would like to know what the Bible is about, and learn who Love is.

My motivation came from a young man named Rob. Rob and my son, Chuck, were best friends in high school. They did a lot of things together including tearing down cars and fixing them again, building a go-cart, having Dr. Pepper breakfasts, and traveling to and from school and work.

One summer they went to <u>Youth For Christ</u> summer camp at the New Jersey shore. There they both accepted Jesus into their lives. Upon returning home they began attending church together. Chuck had grown up going to church, but Rob had not attended Sunday School until this time. In Sunday School they began talking about the resurrection of Jesus, but Rob did not understand what this meant.

I believe there are many 'Robs' who would like to know about Jesus. It will probably only take a few hours to read this book. My desire is that it will help many to know and love this wonderful person, Jesus, who was willing to die for each one of us, then the resurrection happened, and Jesus arose from the dead. And now, HE LIVES and is preparing a place for those of us who believe in Him, where we will live with Him forever.

Chapter 1

In The Beginning

God existed before the very beginning of time. The earth at that time was formless and empty. God spent six days creating the world – light, darkness, day and night, dry land, seas, trees, grass and flowers, summer and winter, sun, moon and stars, birds, fish, animals, and man. God was very pleased with all that He had created and God rested on the seventh day.

Everything God had made was perfect. There was nothing to ruin the beauty and loveliness of all He had made. God named the man He had created, Adam. Now, Adam needed a friend, so God gave him a woman and Adam named her Eve.

God gave Adam and Eve a beautiful garden in which to live. Everything was beautiful and perfect in this garden, God named Eden. In the middle of the garden was a tree with fruit; the tree was called the "tree of the knowledge of good and evil." God told them they could eat any food in the Garden of Eden except the fruit from this tree, for if they did they would surely die.

Complete happiness was theirs until one day when the tempter, Satan, in the form of a snake, told Eve that if she ate of the "tree of the knowledge of good and evil" she would become more intelligent. She would know the difference between good and bad. Eve decided to eat some of the fruit. She gave some to Adam also.

They had disobeyed God. This disobedience broke the perfect harmony they had between God and man. Anything done or left undone that breaks harmony between God and man, is sin. God punished Adam and Eve for their sin by sending them out of the beautiful Garden of Eden. Now there would be thorns and thistles and they would have to work to grow food for themselves. Life on earth would now end in death, because sin leads to death.

Adam and Eve had a son whom they named Cain. Later they had another son, Abel. As these boys grew up, Cain worked as a farmer and Abel was a shepherd. Cain took some of the fruits that he raised, as a gift offering to God, but Abel took his best sheep as his offering. God was pleased with Abel's offering but not with Cain's. This made Cain angry so he killed his brother. God punished Cain by not allowing his crops to grow any more.

Adam and Eve had more children, grandchildren and great grandchildren. Many of these began to live lives not pleasing to God. They were not obeying Him anymore. There was a lot of violence. God became very upset with the people living such sinful lives. In fact, it was so bad that God wished He had not created man at the beginning. Therefore, God decided to destroy all people, birds, and animals.

Chapter 2

Noah

There lived one man who loved God and obeyed Him. His name was Noah. God asked Noah to build a large boat called an ark. God told him exactly how big to make it. Again, Noah obeyed God even though he could not understand why they would ever need such a big boat, since they had never had any rain. Always before, a mist had come up from the ground to water the earth. It took Noah many years to build the ark. People made fun of him, but Noah loved God and did as God commanded him to do.

When the ark was completed, God asked Noah to take his wife, their three sons and their wives, and a pair of each animal, male and female, into the ark with him. He was also to take seven pairs of animals that could be eaten, or used as offerings. Noah was to take enough food for his family and for all the animals that would be in the ark. Noah did as God had said and when they were all in the ark, God shut the door.

For the first time in history, it began to rain. The rain kept on for forty days and forty nights until the whole earth was flooded. Noah and his family and the animals with them were safe in the ark. All the other people and animals were destroyed. There was water on the earth for 150 days and each day as the wind blew it was drying up the water. As the water began to recede, the ark came to rest on Mount Ararat. In about three months they could see the tops of other mountains. Noah waited another forty days for the water to recede. Then Noah opened the window of the ark and let a raven out. The raven flew around until he found a place to land and never returned to the ark. A bit later he sent out a dove, but the dove returned, because he could find no place to make a nest. Seven days later he sent the dove out again. This time the dove returned with a fig leaf in his beak. Noah waited another week and sent the dove out a third time. This time the dove did not return, so Noah knew it was safe to let the animals out of the ark.

Noah, his family, and the animals got out of the ark and walked on dry land. He was so thankful to God for saving their lives that he built an altar to God. He burned one of the best animals on it as an offering of thanks to God. God told Noah that He would never again rid the earth of all its' people and every living thing upon it by a flood. As a sign of this promise to us, God put a rainbow in the sky.

Chapter 3

Abraham

Ten generations later there lived a man named Abram. Abram was a good man. He loved God and was obedient to Him. God told Abram that He would bless him, give him many descendants, and make him famous if he would continue to obey Him. God changed Abram's name to Abraham, which means, 'Father of Many Nations'. For a long time Abraham and his wife Sarah did not have children. Abraham began to wonder how God was going to bless him with many descendants if he didn't even have any children.

God asked Abraham to move from Haran to wherever he would show him. He would continue to bless him and make his name great. He would have lots of land, and descendants as numerous as the stars in the sky.

Abraham remained obedient to God. He took his nephew Lot with him, and they left Haran. Both Abraham and Lot had lots of cattle and sheep and herdsmen to tend to their animals. The herdsmen began to quarrel with each other, so Abraham told Lot to choose which land he wanted and he would take the other land. Lot saw some of the land had plenty of water and good grazing for his animals, so he chose that land which was close to the city of Sodom. The people of Sodom were very wicked. God said he was going to destroy the cities of Sodom and Gomorrah because of their wickedness. Abraham knew Lot lived in the city of Sodom so he asked God if he would spare the city if there were fifty good men there. God said he would but he couldn't find that many. So Abraham asked if he could spare it if He found forty, then thirty, and twenty. God told him he wouldn't destroy it if he even found ten. That evening two men, who were God's angels, went to Lot and told him to take his wife and two daughters and leave and do not look back. However, as they were leaving, Lot's wife did look back and she turned into a block of salt.

When Abraham was one hundred years old, he and Sarah finally had a son whom they named Isaac. God wanted to see if Abraham still loved him and would still obey Him. He asked Abraham to take his son, Isaac, up into the mountain and kill him as a sacrifice there. Abraham did not want to do this, but he knew he must obey God; then just as he raised the knife to kill Isaac, God stopped him. Abraham looked behind him and there was a sheep caught by his horns in a bush nearby. Abraham took the sheep and used it as a burnt offering to God instead of his son, Isaac. God knew then that Abraham loved Him even more than his own son and enough that he would do anything God would ask.

Chapter 4

Jacob

When Abraham's son, Isaac, grew to be a man, he married a woman named Rebecca. They had twin sons whom they named Esau and Jacob. Isaac was partial to Esau because he was his elder son, but Rebecca was more partial to Jacob. As Isaac became an old man and could no longer see, he wanted to give his family blessing to Esau. He asked Esau, who was a hunter, to go get a deer and fix it for him to eat, then he would give him his blessing.

While Esau was out hunting, his mother was telling Jacob to go in to his father and trick his father into believing he was Esau. She told him to take the goat she had prepared for him then he would receive his father's blessing. So Jacob received the blessing that was meant for Esau. This made Esau very angry and wanted to kill Jacob.

Rebecca, realizing that Esau was very angry with Jacob, asked Jacob to go live with her brother Laban in Haran, until Esau would no longer be angry. So Jacob left and when night came he slept out under the stars. That night he had a dream of a ladder reaching to heaven with angels going up and down on the ladder. There God told Jacob that he, like his grandfather Abraham, was going to have lots of land and many descendants.

Jacob continued his journey. He came to a well and met some men from Haran. He asked them if they knew Laban. They said they did and that Laban's daughter, Rachel, would soon be bringing her sheep to be watered there. When Jacob saw Rachel he told her who he was. She ran home to tell her father that his sister's son, Jacob, was there. Laban invited him to stay with them. Jacob started working for Laban who said, "...since you are my relative I should pay you. What wages would you like to have?" Now, Laban had two daughters, Leah, the elder and Rachel, the younger. Jacob loved Rachel so he told Laban he would work for him seven years if he could have Rachel for his wife. The agreement was made and Jacob worked for seven years and got married. However, Laban had given Leah to be his wife instead of Rachel because he said it is tradition for the older daughter to marry before the younger. Jacob definitely felt tricked, but Laban told him if he would work another seven years he could also have Rachel. So, Jacob worked another seven years for Rachel to become his wife. He continued working for Laban for a total of twenty years. Then God told Jacob to gather his family and his animals and go back to his homeland.

Jacob did not know if Esau was still angry with him and as he was traveling homeward he looked and saw that Esau was coming toward them with four hundred men. Jacob divided his family and animals into groups. He put the handmaids and their children in the front group, Leah and her children in the second group and Rachel and their son, Joseph, at the very end. Then Jacob went ahead of them all and met up with Esau. They hugged and kissed each other and cried. They had forgiven one another and were happy to see each other.

Jacob and Rachel later had another son they named Benjamin, and now Jacob had a total of 12 sons.

Chapter 5

Joseph

J oseph was Jacob's favorite because he was Rachel's oldest son. Jacob made a beautiful and very colorful coat for Joseph. This made Joseph's brothers very jealous.

Joseph had a dream. He told his brothers that in his dream they were all out in the field when his shock of grain stood up and all their shocks bowed down to his. His brothers asked him if he thought he would reign over them or have control of them.

Then, Joseph had another dream where the sun, moon and eleven stars bowed to him. This made the brothers even more jealous and they hated him even more.

One day, Joseph's brothers were out tending sheep. Jacob told Joseph to go find them and see if everything was all right. When the brothers saw him coming, they conspired against him to kill him. One of the brothers named Rueben, didn't want to kill him, so instead, they decided to take his beautiful colorful coat and throw Joseph into a pit.

After a while they saw some travelers coming toward them who were going to Egypt. Judah, another of the brothers, suggested they sell Joseph to the travelers. That way they could get rid of Joseph without having to have it on their conscience that they killed him. So they sold Joseph to the travelers for twenty pieces of silver.

Later, Reuben, who did not see what they had done to Joseph, looked for him in the pit. When he saw that Joseph was not there, he became alarmed and asked the others where Joseph was. They told him that they sold him and that they had put blood from a goat on his coat to make their father think that a wild animal had eaten him. When they showed it to their father, he believed that Joseph was dead.

In the meantime, the travelers took Joseph along to Egypt, where Joseph lived in the King's Palace. Joseph always did what was asked of him, so he was pleasing both to God and to the people he worked for.

For seven years Joseph worked hard to store up food because the land was very prosperous. Then there were seven years when nothing grew. Joseph had enough stored away for the people in Egypt, but people from nearby countries also came to him for food. Jacob, Joseph's father, was one who also needed to buy food. He sent his sons, all except Benjamin, the youngest, and now Jacob's favorite, to buy corn in Egypt.

When they arrived, Joseph recognized them but they did not recognize him. Joseph decided to test them. He told them he wouldn't give them any corn because they were spies and had come to check out how poor the land was. But the brothers kept insisting that they were not spies. They told him that they were all brothers and that one had been left at home with their father. Joseph wanted to make sure that

Benjamin was alive and that they had not treated Benjamin like he himself had been treated. He told them he was going to keep Simeon, the second oldest, until they come back with their youngest brother. The brothers thought they were being punished for what they had done to Joseph years earlier, but they still did not recognize Joseph.

Joseph kept Simeon and gave the brothers corn and put their money right back into the bags of corn. After they had traveled a good distance, they stopped to feed their donkeys. When they opened a bag of corn, they found the money they had used to pay for it. The brothers were afraid, thinking perhaps, and hoping it had just been a mistake. But, when they got home they found their money in each bag, not just in one bag. They told their father Jacob, that the Leader of Egypt called them spies, that he kept Simeon, and that they must take Benjamin along back to get Simeon. Jacob was very distressed because he was afraid that something would happen to Benjamin as it had to Joseph. Jacob would not let them go until they were out of grain again. Finally, he let them go and take Benjamin, as well as the money they had found in their sacks. He also told them to pay double the price that Egypt was asking for the corn.

When Joseph saw his brothers coming, he saw Benjamin was with them, so he ordered a meal prepared for them. After they ate, Joseph commanded that the sacks of corn be filled for his brothers and again all the money shall be put back into each sack. Also, Joseph's silver cup was to be put into Benjamin's sack.

After all the brothers left, including Simeon, Joseph sent a steward to catch up with them and accuse them of stealing the money and the cup. Joseph said that the one who had his silver cup in his sack would become his servant. When they discovered the cup was in Benjamin's sack, they became very upset. Judah pleaded with Joseph to allow Benjamin to go home with them because it would cause his father's death if he didn't take him home. Judah told Joseph that his father lost one of his sons to wild animals and couldn't bear losing his youngest son, too.

Joseph asked his brothers if their father was still living. They told him that he was living and in good health. Then they bowed down to him, which made Joseph's dream come true.

Joseph, seeing and hearing all of this was very touched and began crying. He told them who he was. He told them not to feel guilty for what they had done to him, because God had planned it this way so that he could supply them with food during the famine. Joseph told them to go home and get their father. Tell him that Joseph is alive.

Joseph wanted his father and his brothers with their families all to move to Egypt. The King, who loved Joseph, was pleased with this idea, so he supplied wagons and everything they would need to move to Egypt.

When the brothers returned to Canaan, where Jacob and his family lived, they told Jacob that Joseph was alive and he wanted them to move to Egypt. He, and all his sons and their families took their animals and all their belongings and moved to Egypt. Now the descendants of Abraham were living in Egypt and just as God had promised, they increased in number.

To sum it up, Abraham and Sarah had one son, Isaac. Isaac had two sons, one of which was Jacob who had twelve sons. Later, the nation of Jacob, or Israel, as he was also known, was divided into twelve tribes, each being named after one of the twelve sons of Israel. These and their descendants became known as the Children of Israel, or the Israelites.

...e was darkness, boils, hail, and enough locusts to cover ...arth. There were ten plagues in all. The last plague ...ath of the firstborn of man and animal. All those ...uld kill a lamb and put the blood of the lamb on ...orposts, God would save from this plague. When ...angel saw the blood on the doorposts, he would ...nd there would be no deaths in that household. ...e first Passover and each year the Children of ...o celebrate the Passover as the day that God ...en people, the Children of Israel, out of the ...y and Egyptian rule. The Children of Israel ...ble. Jews of today still celebrate the Passover

...e oldest child of all the Egyptians died, ...uch disturbed and told Moses to take the ...d get out of the land. So the Israelites ...rney out of the land of Egypt and their ...t to the Red Sea, God told Moses to ...he water. As he did so, God divided ...dry path for the Israelites to pass

...hanged his mind. He didn't want ...res they had. He sent his men to ...hem back. When the Israeli... ...and the king's men be... ...ters behind the Isr... ...horses were dr... ...ow God h... ...Egypti...

...they ...
...as ...
...the d ...
...hav ...
...ther for
...them God
...A day
...them and
...jewelr just
...placed God,
...believe venth
...He told
...people q er for
...God y angry
...down the e hit the
...the golde Moses to
...they had d er for the
...of stone on
...ground and continued
...they had for eople, the
...(Israel) so so omised to
...ground it into ying a pillar
...made the peo re to guide
...more tablets of
...would give him

Chapter 6

Moses and the Children of Israel

As time went on, a new king was appointed in Egypt. This king did not remember Joseph, so he and his family were not given the privileges they had received before. The new king saw that the descendants of Jacob, or Israel, were becoming a large and strong group. He decided these people should become slaves of the Egyptian people. He made them work very hard. The Israelites kept increasing in number and strength, which caused great disturbance to the king. He thought he could stop the increasing number by a decree, or law, that every Israelite baby boy must be killed.

One day a baby boy was born to an Israelite family. His mother saw that he was a healthy, good looking son. She decided to hide him in hopes they would not find and kill him. After three months, she could hide him no longer. She made a small basket boat and put him into the river. His sister, Miriam, hid herself in the bushes nearby, so she could see what they would do with the baby when they found him.

The king's daughter went to the river to bathe. She saw the basket and sent one of her maids to get it. When she opened the basket, she saw the baby. He was crying and she felt sorry for him. She saw the baby was an Israelite. Then Miriam came and asked the king's daughter if she would like for her to get someone to take care of the baby. Miriam went after her own mother. The king's daughter asked the baby's own mother to take care of him, although she did not know that the woman was his mother.

As the baby grew older, the king's daughter took him to live with her and be her son. She named him Moses, meaning, 'drawn out', because she said she drew him out of the water.

When Moses grew up and became a man, God asked him through a voice in a flaming bush that did not burn, to become the leader and spokesman for the Children of Israel. He was to help them out of their troublesome situation of being hard-driven slaves. Moses did not feel he was capable of doing this. God assured him that He would help him all times.

Just as Noah, Abraham, and Joseph obeyed G Moses. He told the Children of Israel that Go to take them out of this land of slavery. Mo Egyptian king, but the king would no told Moses to take a rod and smite th it would turn to blood. Then God land, but still the king would no leave. God sent more plagues includi and animals dying, but none of the Israe

---

God wanted them to have a safe place to keep the Ten Commandments (law or covenant) He had given them. He asked them to make a chest (ark) and line it with gold. It was called the 'Ark of the Covenant'. On top of the ark God told them to place a mercy seat. Two angels with spread wings, one on each end, were to hover over the mercy seat. They were to put rings on the sides and gold lined poles through the rings so they could carry the ark with these poles. Then they were to build a place of worship in which to keep the 'Ark of the Covenant'. They were to have a tent with two rooms separated by a curtain or veil. The one room was called The Holy Place. Only priests could be in that room called 'The Most Holy' or 'Holy of Holies'. This was the room where the ark was kept and only the High Priest could enter that room.

The priests were chosen from the descendants of Levi, one of the twelve sons of Jacob (Israel). They were in charge of carrying the 'Ark of the Covenant'. They were also to transport, set up, and repair the tent. They were to prepare the burnt offerings of thanks and sacrifices of sin.

The priests would build an altar built of stones and burn an animal or bird, which was supposed to be perfect, without any defect. These animals' lives were sacrificed for the peoples' sins. Then God would forgive His people.

When the pillar of cloud or pillar of fire moved, that meant that God wanted the Children of Israel to move on. Each time they would take along the 'ark' and the tent of worship, or tabernacle, as it was called. Because the 'ark' symbolized God's presence, it was considered very holy. No one dared touch the 'ark' itself or they would die. This was to show or signify the holiness of God.

For forty years the Children of Israel moved through the wilderness this way. God loved them very much. They were His chosen people. They had many rules and regulations which were to teach them that God was in total control of everything. He wanted them to obey and worship only Him. He wanted to lead them back into Canaan, the 'Promised Land', for His chosen people.

One day as they neared Canaan, God told Moses to send twelve spies into Canaan to see what the country looked like. Two of these spies were Caleb and Joshua. They and ten others, all direct descendants of Jacob and Abraham, were sent to check out this land. They spent forty days checking out this 'Promised Land'. They returned telling the Israelites that it was a magnificent country with plenty of food. They found some clusters of grapes so large that two men were needed to carry one cluster. The spies also reported that the people there are very powerful and very large, like giants. Most of the spies were afraid to try to conquer the land, but Caleb was sure they could do it with God's help. The people began to complain again. And again, some of them wished they had been left in Egypt as slaves. Joshua and Caleb assured the people that the country was a wonderful place and that God would see them return to Canaan safely. They told them not to be afraid because God would protect them.

Chapter 7

Joshua and the Children of Israel

Moses lived to be 120 years old, but he died before he would lead the Children of Israel to the 'Promised Land'. God asked Joshua to become their leader now. Forty years had passed since they had left Egypt as slaves. Joshua led them to the Jordan River which separated them from the 'Promised Land'. On the other side of the river was the City of Jericho. Joshua sent two spies to Jericho to check out the city. When they came back, they told Joshua that the people there are afraid of them because they had heard how the God of Israel had led them out of Egypt and that He was more powerful than their gods.

God wanted the Children of Israel to know that He was leading Joshua just as He had led Moses. To get to the 'Promised Land' they had to cross the Jordan River. He told Joshua to have the men who were carrying the 'Ark of the Covenant' to go before the people. As soon as they would step into the Jordan River the waters would divide and they would go across on dry ground, just as they had with Moses at the Red Sea.

After crossing the Jordan River they came to the City of Jericho and found it had a huge wall built around it. God told Joshua to march around the city one time each day for six days. On the seventh day they were to march around the city seven times and then the priests should blow their trumpets. While they blew the trumpets, the rest of the people should shout and make noises. When the Children of Israel did as God told them to do, the walls around Jericho fell down and the Israelites seized the city. This was only the beginning of seizing the land of Canaan for the Children of Israel. God wanted them to understand that He was in control and that they should obey Him always. There were times that they didn't obey Him and He would punish them by not allowing victory in battle.

Through all this, God was still keeping His promise or covenant that He had made to Abraham, saying his descendants would be many. The Children of Israel were continuing to increase in number. They were to keep on obeying God, His commandments and laws. They didn't set up their new empire with a king, but they had judges to rule and teach them all the laws.

During the time the judges were ruling in Canaan, now called Israel, there was another famine where they did not have enough to eat. A man named Elimelech took his wife, Naomi, and their two sons to Moab to look for food. While they were in Moab their sons married wives named Orpha and Ruth. As time went on, Elimelech and their two sons died. One day Naomi decided to move back to her homeland, back to the Children of Israel. She asked Orpha and Ruth to return to their families in Moab because she too was going back home. Both daughters-in-law hated to leave her, but Orpha did go back to her family. Ruth told Naomi she wanted to go with her to Israel and worship God as Naomi did.

When Naomi and Ruth got back to the City of Bethlehem, there was a wealthy farmer named Boaz, who was also a direct descendant of Abraham. After Boaz would harvest his crop, Ruth would go into the fields to gather what was left. When Boaz saw Ruth, and knew that she was trying to help her mother-in-law Naomi, he told his servants to leave extra grain in the field for Ruth to gather. Later Boaz married Ruth and they were great grandparents to David, who would be the Children of Israel's second king.

The Children of Israel had been under the ruling of God and the judges, but they wanted to have a king like the other people around them. One of the judges whose name was Samuel was very upset that they would want an earthly king instead of seeing God as their king. God, too, did not want this, but the people kept insisting this was what they wanted, so God told Samuel to go ahead and give them a king.

Chapter 8

Kings

God chose a man named Saul to be their first king. He was a descendant of Abraham's great grandson, Benjamin, Joseph's younger brother. Saul was a good man and obeyed God. He had a son named Jonathan. Now Saul was sure Jonathan would be king after he died. But God had other plans. God wanted David, who was another descendant of Abraham and Boaz, to be the next king. David had grown up as a shepherd spending many hours watching sheep and singing songs to God. Many of the songs he sang were written down in a book called *The Psalms*. David also played musical instruments, one of which was a harp. David used these talents to obey and please God.

David and Jonathan were good friends. Jonathan knew it was God's plan for David to be the next king, so that was how Jonathan wanted it, but his father, Saul, did not. It made Saul very jealous and angry so he decided he must kill David.

During Saul's reign as king, the Philistines and the Israelites were at war. At this time there was a giant of a man

Chapter 9

Babylon (Excile) and Daniel

The Kingdom of Israel was divided into twelve tribes. Each tribe was given the name of one of Jacob's twelve sons.

Israel kept growing in number and gaining land. In the newly gained land were people who worshiped many other gods instead of the true God, the one who delivered them from slavery in Egypt. The Israelites began worshiping some of these gods too, all the while ignoring the prophets' warning. When they would forget the true God and worship other gods, they often lost battles or had other hardships in their lives.

One of the battles lost was to Babylon because they would not listen to the prophets and turn back to God. The king of Babylon, Nebuchadnezzar, seized Jerusalem. He took many of the people captive and brought them to Babylon. Most of these people had been worshiping other gods. The king particularly wanted the fittest of the young

n, the most skillful and intelligent. Among those chosen
ere Shadrach, Meshach, and Abednego. These young men
were believers in the true God and obedient to Him. The
king, who did not believe in God, was well pleased with
these young men.

King Nebuchadnezzar built a large image of gold.
When it was finished he had a day of dedication. On that
day he commanded that when the music began, everyone
there was to bow down and worship this image. He told
them if they didn't bow down they would be thrown into a
very hot furnace.

Shadrach, Mechach, and Abednego would only worship
the true God, their God. They would not bow down and
orship this idol. The king gave them a second chance, but
till the young men would not bow. They told the king that
their God could deliver them out of the fiery furnace, but
if He didn't, they still would not bow to a different god.
When the music began again and Shadrach, Mechach, and
Abednego would not bow down, the king commanded the
furnace be heated seven times hotter than usual. The young
men were bound and thrown into the furnace. The men that
threw them in, died because of the intense heat.

As King Nebuchadnezzar watched, he said he thought
they threw three men into the furnace, but he could see
four of them; and the fourth one had the form like the
Son of God. Then the king ordered the young men to
come out of the furnace. The king and those around them
said they didn't smell burned, nor was even a hair on their
heads singed. Then the king said, "Blessed be the God of
Shadrach, Mechach, and Abednego". He ordered no one to
say anything against their God.

Some time later Darius became king of Babylon and chose one hundred and twenty princes to preside over the kingdom. Then he chose three presidents over the princes. The first president Daniel, also from Israel, was one of the king's favorites because of his skills and intelligence. However, some of the princes were jealous and wanted to find fault with Daniel, but they couldn't find any, so they got King Darius to make a firm decree that no one was to pray, asking anything from any god or man, except the king. If anyone would break this law, or decree, they would be thrown into a den of lions. King Darius did not realize they were doing this to get rid of his friend Daniel. Daniel was true to God and prayed to Him every day. King Darius had to stay with his law and had to throw Daniel into the lion's den. That night the king could not sleep, he was very worried for Daniel. Early in the morning the king went to check on Daniel. He asked, "Has your God been able to save you?" When Daniel answered that God had saved him, the king was overjoyed. Yes, God was protecting Daniel and wouldn't let the lions harm him.

Chapter 10

Prophets

While the Children of Israel were in exile in Babylon, God would send prophets to them to remind them of Himself, and to tell them what would happen if they didn't turn back to God and obey Him. Some of these prophets were: Amos, a fearless man; tenderhearted Hosea; Jeremiah, the man of many sorrows; and Ezekiel, who kept up the courage of the people during their exile into Babylon.

Another one of the prophets was named Jonah. God told Jonah to go to Ninevah and warn the people there, that in forty days they would be overthrown unless they turn away from their evil doings. They must begin obeying God again. Jonah did not want to go, so instead, he went by ship which was headed to Joppa. God caused a high wind to come upon the waters and they were afraid the ship would sink. They threw everything overboard to help lighten the ship. Still, the storm continued. Finally, Jonah told them he was running away from God. They asked him what they should do with him and he said, "throw me overboard."

When they threw him overboard the storm ceased. God provided a big fish to swallow Jonah. He was in the fish for three days and three nights. Jonah prayed to God and admitted he was wrong, so God caused the fish to vomit Jonah out onto dry land. Jonah went to Ninevah and spoke to the Children of Israel. They repented of their evil doings and started worshiping the true God again.

Another prophet of God was Isaiah. He prophesied much about the coming of a King who would deliver them out of the hands of their enemies. This King was to be the Messiah, the Savior to save the world. He was to be a descendant of Abraham and He was to be born in Bethlehem.

There were fourteen generations from Abraham to King David and from King David to their captivity into Babylon was another fourteen generations. Then another fourteen generations later, Jesus the King, about whom Isaiah had prophesied, was born.

Chapter 11

Jesus' Birth and Life

Jesus was the Son of God. God wanted Jesus to live on earth for a period of time to teach us who He was and how to live like Him. In His power, God worked this out by having a young woman named Mary become pregnant through the Holy Spirit (God in Spirit). Mary's husband, Joseph, was another direct descendant of Abraham and David. This brought about God's promise to Abraham, that the Messiah would be one of his descendants, and the prophecy that Isaiah prophesied, that Jesus would be in the lineage of David.

God, through an angel, told Mary, and later told Joseph, what His plans were; that they were to be the parents of His son, the King and Savior of the world. At that time, the Israelites were under Roman rule. They were looking and hoping for a king who would relieve them from the strong hard rule of the Roman Empire. Jesus did not set up an earthly kingdom, but instead, was preparing a heavenly kingdom.

One day Caesar Augustus, ruler of the Roman Empire, decided that all the world should be taxed. In order to do this, each family had to go to the city from which their family originated, to be counted and taxed. Joseph and Mary lived in Nazareth where Joseph was a carpenter. However, because they were from the family of King David, they had to go to Bethlehem, which is also called the City of David. From Nazareth to Bethlehem was almost seventy-five miles. They made the trip by donkey, their means of transportation in those days.

Many other people went to Bethlehem for the same reason, so all the inns (hotels) were full. When Joseph and Mary arrived they had no place to sleep. Finally, an owner of an inn told them of a stable where animals were kept. They could sleep in there for the night. They accepted the place and that night Baby Jesus was born, just as Isaiah had prophesied.

The night Jesus was born there were shepherds watching their sheep on a hillside. An angel came to them and told them that Jesus was born. While he was telling them this, there was a bright light in the sky with many angels praising God for this wonderful event. After the angels left, the shepherds wanted to go see the baby, Jesus. They went to Bethlehem and found Mary and Joseph, with baby Jesus lying in a manger where Mary had fixed a bed for Him. The Shepherds were so excited they wanted to tell everyone.

This was the beginning of God's new plan. Ever since Adam and Eve had sinned, all humans have been sinful. Before this sin, there had been perfect harmony between God and people, but sin separated people from God so that God had to provide a way back to harmony. In order to do this, God said that blood must be shed. At the first Passover, the Children of Israel had to kill a lamb and put the blood on the door posts, this was the shed blood, a sign for God to save them. During the time of kings and prophets, the Israelites would kill animals and burn them on an altar as a sign of repentance, being sorry for their sins and turning back to obeying God. Now God had another plan, a plan that included Jesus, His son.

Jesus, being a Jew, would celebrate the Passover with His parents annually. This was to remind the people how God had brought them out of Egypt and how His death angel had 'passed over' the houses where the blood was sprinkled on the door posts.

The Passover was held in Jerusalem. Each year they would travel to Jerusalem for this celebration. On the way home from the Passover celebration, when Jesus was twelve years old, His parents assumed that He was with the other children who were traveling with them. At the end of the day, they looked for Jesus, but He wasn't with the group. They went back to Jerusalem to look for Him. They found Him in the temple, the house of worship. He was talking with doctors and highly educated men. They were amazed that Jesus knew so much and could answer many of their questions. Mary asked Jesus why He had not gone along with the group when they started home. Jesus told her that He was doing the work that God, His Father, had sent Him to do. Then they all left to go back to Nazareth. Mary understood what Jesus was doing because she knew He was the Son of God.

Jesus grew and learned and helped His earthly father with carpenter work. He studied the books of law written in

Moses' time. When He was about thirty years old He went into the wilderness where He could be alone. Jesus wanted to spend some time in prayer (talking to God) to prepare Himself for the work God had sent Him to earth to do.

He was in the wilderness for forty days without anything to eat. Satan, the devil, came to Jesus to tempt Him. Satan told Jesus that if He really was the Son of God, He should command the stones to be made into bread, then He would have something to eat. Jesus told Satan that it was written in the law that man does not live by bread alone but by every word that God says.

Then Satan took Jesus on a high mountain, and tempting Him again, told Jesus that if He would worship and obey him, Jesus would have power over all that He could see. Jesus told Satan to leave, for the law says you are not to worship or serve anyone or anything except God.

Satan did not give up. He took Jesus up on a pinnacle, a high place in the temple, and told him to jump off, that God would save Him if He really was God's Son. Again, Jesus answered him from what He had learned in studying the Law of Moses. He told him that the law says you are not to tempt God. Then Satan left Jesus alone.

After Jesus had been tempted by Satan, He began His ministry which God had sent Him to do. He chose twelve men to help Him and asked them to be His followers (disciples). He spent much time teaching the twelve disciples what they were to do after Jesus left the earth. The disciples did not realize that Jesus would be with them only a short time.

To try and teach His disciples and others who He was, and why He was on earth; Jesus performed miracles, something man cannot do without God's help. The first miracle of Jesus was at a wedding in Cana where He was a guest. His mother Mary was also at the wedding. Mary told Jesus they had no more wine to give to the guests. Jesus told His disciples to take the six empty water pots of stone and fill them with water. When they did what Jesus said to do, the water turned into wine. When the disciples saw this, they believed that Jesus was truly God's Son. Jesus not only wanted to teach the twelve disciples, but He wanted everyone to know about who He was and about His mission.

There were many people who would gather around to hear His teaching. One day over 5,000 people got together to listen to Jesus. When it came time to eat, the disciples didn't know how they were going to feed so many people. Jesus asked if anyone in the crowd had anything to eat. A young boy had brought his lunch of five small loaves of bread and two small fish. He was willing to share his lunch, but that would not be enough to feed that many people. Jesus took the lunch, blessed it, and began breaking it into pieces and putting it into baskets. Then the disciples gave food to the people until they had all they wanted to eat. When they were done eating, they still had twelve baskets of food left. This was another miracle Jesus performed to show people that He really was the Son of God.

Sometimes Jesus would take time away from the crowds and spend time alone with the twelve disciples. It was one of those times when they asked Him how to pray to God, who is also our Father. He told them to say, "Our Father which art in heaven, Hallowed be thy name. Thy kingdom come. Thy will be done in earth, as it is in heaven. Give us this day our daily bread. And forgive us our debts, (trespasses) as we forgive our debtors (those who trespass against us). And lead us not into temptation, but deliver us from evil: For thine is the kingdom, and the power, and the glory, forever. Amen." Matthew 6:9b-13 KJV *Words in parenthesis are added.*

Jesus went from city to city telling them that He was the Messiah, the King they were waiting for. Since they were looking for a king who would take the throne and overthrow the Roman Empire, many people did not believe Jesus. However, Jesus kept right on teaching and performing miracles. He taught them that when Moses wrote the Ten Commandments, they were to obey those laws, but now that He had come to earth, He also wanted them to do things out of love, mercy and forgiveness. Jesus brought an all new way of life. He had come to earth to rid people of some of the harsh man-made Jewish laws. He wanted people to live in unity, harmony and love as they did when the earth was first created. He had come so that people would no longer need to go to the High Priest, who would go into the Holy of Holies, to speak to God for them. People would now be able to talk to God through Jesus. This is why when people pray (talk to God) they often end, "In Jesus' name, Amen."

As Jesus traveled along, He saw many people who were sick, blind, or lame and He would take time out to heal them. Because of these miracles, more people believed that He was the Son of God.

One day a Jewish ruler came to Jesus and told Him that his daughter was dying. The ruler, Jairus, believed that if Jesus would come to his house Jesus could heal her. Jesus went to Jairus' house, and on His way a woman who had been sick for twelve years touched just the hem of Jesus' robe. She believed that she could be healed this way. Immediately

ⁿis robe
it could
ᵈ gathered
.aling power
ᵉn healed said
.t because of her

ᵉn they got into the

of Jesus' friends,

Jesus often spent

.ha away teaching,

ᵉ knew Jesus

quickly. Jesus

ᵉ could teach

Son of God,

ᵈ Martha,

sisters told

not have

went to

ᵉ out of

people

ᵒn of

.me

.a

.an, someone came

died, so don't bother

.im not to be afraid but

.s got to Jairus' house, the

.e and the child had already

.ne was only sleeping and he

.ead throughout the area so that

.d about and believed in Jesus.

.. Jesus had been teaching many people

He told the disciples to get into the boat

.in them later. After the crowds of people

.sus went up into the mountain to talk to His

.ther. Jesus spent a great deal of time talking to

.e mountains alone.

.ring the night, a wind storm arose and the disciples

.afraid. Jesus saw they were afraid so He walked on the

water to the boat. When they saw Him, they were afraid again because they thought he was a ghost. Jesus talked to them. One of the disciples named Peter said, "If it is really you, Jesus, ask me to come to you." Jesus told Peter to walk to Him. Peter stepped out of the boat and started walking on the water until he thought of the storm and lost faith, then he began to sink. Immediately Jesus helped him, but

asked him why he had doubted Him. T
boat and Jesus calmed the storm.

In the town of Bethany lived some
Mary, Martha and their brother Lazarus.
time with them. One day while Jesus wa
Lazarus became very sick. Mary and Mar
could heal him so they sent for Him to com
already knew this was going to happen so H
and let people know who He really was – the
sent by God.

By the time Jesus came back to Mary ar
Lazarus had died and they had buried him. The
Jesus that if He had been there, Lazarus would
died. Jesus loved them and he loved Lazarus. He
the grave and cried. Then He told Lazarus to com
the grave. When Lazarus came out, many of the
believed Jesus truly was who He said He was, the
the Living God.

Everywhere Jesus went He healed people and perfor
many miracles. Some people believed Him when He
He was God's son, yet others refused to believe Him. Soi
wanted to catch Jesus lying or breaking one of the laws, th
way they would have a reason to get rid of the man who wa
becoming so popular among the people. They would ask
Jesus all kinds of questions so they could find Him guilty of
something, but Jesus always had a truthful answer for them.

Just before the yearly celebration of Passover, when Jesus
had been on earth for about thirty-three years, the disciples
borrowed a donkey and brought it to Jesus. They put some
of their clothes on the donkey for Jesus to sit on. Jesus
rode on the donkey into Jerusalem. Many people came to

welcome Jesus and to honor and praise Him for the many things He had done for the people. They laid clothes on the path for the donkey to walk on. They also cut branches from the palm trees and laid them in the path while they were singing praises to Jesus. This celebration is known today as Palm Sunday.

The Jewish leaders became very angry because Jesus was given so much attention. They got together to decide how they could get rid of Jesus. They decided not to do it at the Passover Feast because they were afraid there would be a riot. Judas Iscariot, one of the twelve disciples, went to the Jewish leaders and asked them what they would give him if he would help them in their plot. The leaders told him they would give him thirty pieces of silver. Judas began watching for the right time and opportunity to turn Jesus over to them.

Chapter 12

Jesus' Death, Resurrection, and Ascension

On the first day of Passover, Jesus sent Peter and John, two of the disciples, into Jerusalem to find a place and to prepare for the Passover Feast. The feast would consist of lamb, and bread without yeast; which is still the traditional food for the Passover Feast. That evening at the Passover meal, Jesus, knowing His death was getting nearer, wanted the disciples to learn more about Him, His departure, and what they were to do after He wasn't with them anymore. He explained to them there was one among them who would turn Him over to the Jewish authorities to be put to death. Each one asked if he was the one that would betray Jesus, because they loved Him so much they couldn't believe that they could betray Him. Of course, Judas knew that he was the one Jesus was talking about.

At the table, Jesus took a cup of wine and told His disciples, this is a symbol of His blood which He was going to shed. Jesus knew that His time of death was very near. Then He took bread and told them that this symbolized His body which would be put to death soon. He wanted them to drink of the wine and eat of the bread to show that they were a part of Jesus' life and also His death. He told them to do this again after His death to show that they remembered this event.

That same evening, Jesus took a towel and water and washed the disciples' feet. This was a custom of that day to wash their guests' feet. Jesus did this to teach His disciples to love each other enough to be servants of each other. He told them to continue to do these things to remind them of His death and to love each other as much as He loved them. Peter wanted Jesus to know how much he loved Him. He said that he would even die for Jesus. Jesus said to Peter, "Three times before the rooster crows you will deny you even know me." Peter did not want to believe he would ever deny Jesus.

After that, Jesus took his disciples, all except Judas, who had left after the Passover meal, and went to one of His places of quietness called the Garden of Gethsemane so that He could pray to God, His Father. He knew His death was the will of God, but He needed God to help Him through this time. Jesus knew that blood had to be shed to forgive sins. He also knew that all mankind since Adam have sinned and that sin leads to death. Jesus was willing to die so that all people could be forgiven and therefore live forever. God's will was that Jesus would now be slain instead of a lamb, ending animal sacrifices. This meant they would no longer need to kill a lamb at Passover because Jesus, whom God called His perfect, without sin, Holy, Lamb of God, was taking its place. God was willing to give His only Son so that the human race could be saved from their sins and death. Such love!

While Jesus was praying in the Garden of Gethsemane, Judas, the Chief Priests, and other authorities were leaving Jerusalem to get Jesus. When they arrived, Peter realized they had come for Jesus, so he took his sword and cut off a High Priest's servant's ear. Jesus told Peter not to do such things, and then He touched the servant's ear and healed it. He told Peter that in order to fulfill the prophecies that had been made years ago, He must go through with this because it was God's will.

As the soldiers took Jesus, the disciples fled for their lives, but followed at a distance to see what they were going to do with their friend Jesus. While watching and waiting, a servant girl said she thought she had seen Peter with Jesus. Peter denied knowing Him. Later, she said to those standing around that Peter was one of Jesus' followers. Again, Peter denied it. After a while others standing there were saying that he surely was one of Jesus' followers and for the third time he denied knowing Jesus. Immediately he heard the rooster crow, and he remembered what Jesus had said. Peter felt very bad about what he had done. He went outside and cried bitterly.

Judas too, realizing what he had done and that they were actually going to kill Jesus, went and hanged himself.

Meanwhile, the Chief Priests were taking Jesus to the Jewish leaders to be questioned. They asked Him who He was, and Jesus told them that He was Jesus, the Son of God.

Anyone who claimed to be someone that he really wasn't was considered having broken the Jewish law. Since the Jewish leaders did not want to believe who Jesus really was, they said He was guilty of the law of blasphemy.

The leaders then took Jesus to the Roman Governor, Pilate, and told him that Jesus was guilty of blasphemy, saying He is God's Son, the King of the Jews. Pilate asked Him if this was true, that he is the Son of God, King of the Jews, and Jesus said it was so. Pilate could find no fault with Jesus so he sent Him to Herod, King of Galilee. Herod questioned Jesus too, but Jesus didn't answer any questions, so Herod started making fun of Jesus, dressing Him in a robe made for a king just to ridicule Him, and sent Him back to Pilate.

Pilate didn't know what to do with Jesus because the people wanted Him killed, but Pilate couldn't find any wrong that Jesus had done. It was a custom to release a prisoner once a year at Passover time so he asked if they would like to release Jesus or Barabbas, a man in prison for theft and murder. The crowd yelled to release Barabbas. Then Pilate's wife talked with Pilate and told him she had a dream about Jesus; that He was a good man and should be let go. Pilate, again, didn't know what to do because he didn't think Jesus had done anything wrong, but that the Jewish leaders were just jealous of Jesus because He had so many people following Him. Pilate saw there was going to be a riot if he didn't turn Jesus over to them to be killed. He washed his hands saying that he didn't want to take the blame for this innocent man. He still gave Jesus to them to do with as they pleased.

The soldiers took Him to a place called Golgatha or Skull Hill, and nailed Him to a cross which was the way criminals served the death penalty in those days. While Jesus was hanging on the cross, He talked to His mother Mary, who was crying at the foot of the cross. He told her that John, one of Jesus' much loved disciples, was to be her son and to John He said that he was to take Mary as his mother.

About noon, while Jesus was hanging on the cross, it became dark and stayed dark for three hours. After the darkness, Jesus said He was thirsty and they gave Him vinegar. When He tasted the vinegar, Jesus said that His work was finished, He had done what He came to earth for, and then Jesus died. One of the soldiers pierced Jesus' side with a sword to make sure his death was complete.

When Jesus died, the curtain that separated the Holy Place and the Holy of Holies in the temple, was torn in half from top to bottom. Many years before, the prophet Jeremiah, had prophesied that this would happen. This was to symbolize that we no longer need a High Priest to go to the Holy of Holies to talk to God for us; now Jesus would be our intercessor between us and God. Oh, the extreme love Jesus had for us to be willing to go through this suffering to death so that our sins could be forgiven!!

A man named Joseph, who was also a follower of Jesus, asked Pilate if he could bury Jesus' body in the tomb on his land. Pilate didn't know that Joseph was Jesus' follower, so he told him he could go ahead and bury the body in that tomb.

Many people, seeing all that had happened during the time Jesus was on the cross crucified, began to realize for the first time that Jesus was actually who He had said He was, the Son of God. They saw that the things which were prophesied actually did come true. Some of the soldiers told Pilate they thought the tomb should be guarded, because Jesus had said He would come to life again on the third day. They were afraid the disciples would steal the body and tell everyone that Jesus had risen from the dead. They sealed the tomb with a large stone and posted guards at the entrance.

Early on the first day of the week following Jesus' death, Mary Magdalene, Jesus' mother, and a close friend of Jesus went to the tomb. They wanted to anoint the body with sweet spices as was the custom of that time. They didn't know how they would roll away the stone. When they got there, they found the stone rolled back from the entrance and an angel was there. The angel told them not to be frightened but that Jesus had risen, had come back to life. "He is alive!" This was the resurrection of Jesus.

The angel told them to go tell the disciples and to meet Jesus in Galilee, where He had told them He would see them again. The women quickly ran to tell the disciples all they had heard and seen. Peter and John, two of the disciples, had to go see for themselves. They still had a hard time believing that He really was alive.

One day while the eleven were together and discussing all that had happened, Thomas, another of the disciples, said he still didn't believe. Jesus showed up in the room and told Thomas to look at His hands and feet and he could see the scars left by the nails they used to put Him on the cross. Then Thomas believed. Jesus told him, "Because you have seen me, you have believed; blessed are they that have not seen yet have believed."

Jesus was with the disciples for forty days explaining the work ahead for them. They were to teach and preach about Jesus, His death and resurrection and all that He had taught them while He was on earth. He would be leaving them to go back to Heaven and be with His Father and to prepare an eternal place for all who believe in Him. Jesus would send the Holy Spirit (Jesus in Spirit) to take His place. The Holy Spirit would not be seen in person as Jesus was, but He would come as their comforter and guide. One day, Jesus told them, He would come back to take them with Him to Heaven and live with Him there forever.

Jesus took the disciples to Bethany and there He asked God to bless the disciples and He lifted His hands and ascended (went up) into Heaven. The disciples were full of joy; they went back to Jerusalem all excited, wanting to tell everyone about Jesus and everything He had done for them. Jesus had told them to wait in Jerusalem for the Holy Spirit.

Chapter 13

The Holy Spirit and The Disciples

While the eleven disciples were waiting in a room in Jerusalem, there was a mighty wind that filled the room and what looked like tongues of fire came upon each of them. They were receiving the Holy Spirit. The Holy Spirit, like the wind, could not be seen but had the power of fire. That day Peter preached to people who had gathered around and many believed in Jesus, who He really was and that He had died, and then rose again and went back to Heaven to be with His Father.

From that day on, the disciples began to preach and teach and make Jesus known to everyone they could. As more and more people began to learn about Jesus, they too would tell others. The government and Jewish church leaders, who did not believe Jesus was the Son of God, began to get very upset at the power these people had, who are now called Christians. They began killing Christians to get rid of them. The Christians believed what Jesus had told them that

He, through the Holy Spirit, would always be with them. This gave them strength and power and even made them willing to die for Jesus' sake, because Jesus had died to save them from eternal death to life after death.

At that time there was a man named Saul who was determined to kill every Christian, to utterly destroy all of them. One day as he was going toward Damascus to destroy the Christians there, a bright light shone down on him. He fell to the ground and he heard a voice asking him why he wanted to kill the Christians. Saul wanted to know who was talking to him in this light that was so bright it made him blind. Jesus told Saul that He was the voice, and asked Saul why he was working so hard against Him. Saul wanted to know what Jesus wanted him to do because he thought he was doing the right thing, but Jesus wanted Saul to be a follower of His, not one to murder those who followed Jesus.

Jesus told Saul to go to Damascus and there he would meet a man named Ananias. So Saul and those with him went into Damascus. There they waited three days; then God spoke to Ananias and told him about Saul. Ananias was afraid to go see Saul because he knew he was killing Christians, however, Jesus assured him that Saul was now also a follower of His. Ananias went to Saul and laid hands on him and immediately Saul could see again. This was the turning point in Saul's life. He began to tell people that this was true about Jesus dying and rising again. He knew Jesus was alive, he had heard him in the bright light, and he believed what he heard. From that time on Saul, now also called Paul, went from city to city and country to country telling everyone, not only the Children of Israel (the Jews), but also other people of different heritages. At first some

Christians were afraid of Paul because of his reputation of killing Christians, but Paul kept right on preaching and teaching till they believed that he had truly changed and was now also following their Jesus.

There were others then, who did not like Paul because of his stand for Jesus. They tried to kill him. Several times they put Paul in prison, but Paul just worked for Jesus there too. One time a prison guard believed in Jesus because of what Paul said and did. While in prison Paul also wrote many letters to his Christian friends in the various cities he had visited previously. He gave many people encouragement and guidelines on how to follow Jesus and be better disciples of Jesus. Some of these letters of advice are found in the New Testament of the *Bible.*

The *Bible* is divided into two parts, the Old Testament where the people lived under the law of Moses and the New Testament where people now live under the love, mercy and grace of God – the God of Heaven and earth, the God who created the earth from the beginning.

Four men who knew who Jesus was, wrote their accounts of life with Jesus while He was on earth. They were Matthew, Mark, Luke and John. They wrote about Jesus' temptations, miracles, His death and how He rose from death to life – the resurrection.

Summary

In summary, first there was perfection, then came sin and because of sin, imperfection; something had to take place to forgive sin. Jesus, by dying and shedding His blood, took away the sin, saving us from death which sin dooms us to, and giving us life forever in Heaven with Him.

We have all sinned, done something wrong against God, so we must be sorry that we have done these things and we must ask God to forgive us those sins. When we tell Him we are sorry for our sins, we repent. In other words, we really want to change from doing evil to doing good.

We must believe that Jesus was born on earth of a virgin, and that He died to forgive our sins. We must believe that He was raised to life again and departed into Heaven to prepare a place for us. Those who believe in Jesus will have life forever with Him in Heaven where there is no sadness, no sickness and no death. Those who do not accept Jesus as God's son and believe in Him will receive their punishment in Hell with Satan and his angels. Hell is described as a lake of fire and total darkness. There will be no love and no happiness there.

There are several things we can do that are helpful if we want to know more about Jesus and what He really wants us to do. One is to read the *Bible*, God's Word. We can also talk to Him, and listen. God, through Jesus, through the Holy Spirit, will reveal many things to us.

We read in the *Bible* in John, chapter three, verse sixteen (John 3:16 NIV), "For God so loved the world that He gave His one and only Son, that whoever believes in Him shall not perish but have eternal life." In Romans chapter ten, verse nine (Romans 10:9 NIV), "That if you confess with your mouth, Jesus is Lord, and believe in your heart that God raised Him from the dead, you will be saved." Jesus said in John, chapter fourteen, verse three (John 14:3 KJV), "If I go and prepare a place for you, I will come again, and receive you unto myself; that where I am, there ye may be also." Jesus is coming back to earth again, although no one knows when, to take us, who believe in Him, to live with Him forever. Jesus said in John 14:6 NIV, "I am the way, and the truth, and the life. No one comes to the Father, except through me."

Now we know, "God is Love. In this was manifested the love of God toward us, because that God sent His only begotten Son into the world, that we might live through Him. Herein is love, not that we loved God, but that He loved us, and sent his Son to be the propitiation (sacrifice) for our sins." I John 4:8b-10 KJV *Words in parenthesis are added.*